Jacob Jay Garfinkel

# Kohelet's Cocktail

## Beyond the Pursuit of Happiness

Meditative Poetry and Illustrations
*Inspired by Ecclesiastes*

 *Illuminated Press*

Author | **Jacob Jay Garfinkel**
Text editor | **Linda Joy Yechiel**
Book Designer | **Hodaya Dahan**

ISBN: 979-8-218-39634-3

———————————————

Contact : MyKohelet@Gmail.com

For Renée

whose love is the constant that defines every page of our journey

# Content

# How Best to Use This Book

## A Guide to Navigating Modern Life with Ancient Wisdom

---

Welcome to a journey through time and wisdom with this contemporary interpretation of the Book of Kohelet, a treasured piece of ancient Hebrew Wisdom literature. This This book, penned over two thousand years ago, still echoes with significance. It is crafted not just as a reading experience but as a guide and a companion for those navigating the complexities and uncertainties of today's world. Here's how to make the most of this timeless wisdom:

**Embrace the Poetry of Life |** This rendition transforms the classical text into accessible, contemporary language, allowing Kohelet's profound messages to resonate more deeply with today's readers. As you explore these pages, you will find guidance, solace, and a refreshing perspective on life's enduring questions.

**Engage with Spontaneity |** Allow serendipity to guide your reading. Open any page randomly to discover a meditation text paired with a visual cue. This approach encourages spontaneous reflection and a deep, personal connection with the teachings.

**Reflect and Meditate |** Use the text and accompanying illustrations to delve into meditation. These elements are designed to aid in your contemplation, helping you to understand the relevance of these ancient teachings in your current life and circumstances.

**Challenge and Grow |** This book invites you to reassess your life's priorities and values. By engaging with Kohelet's wisdom, you are encouraged to shift focus from material pursuits to a life enriched with wisdom, contentment, and spiritual grounding.

By engaging with this book in these ways, you will not only enjoy a literary experience but also embark on a transformative journey that bridges millennia, connecting the ancient wisdom of Kohelet with the challenges and opportunities of the modern era.

**Jacob Jay Garfinkel**
Jerusalem, 5784

Chapter 1

Meditation on **Life's Impermanence**

*Through Jerusalem's delicate night and days,*

*the son of David, the perceptive sage,*

*uttered tales of fleeting woe,*

*of how man's desires ebb and flow.*

*Life's just a breath, gone in a blink.*

*We chase the wind. And then we think,*

*how everything's pointless, a relentless quest.*

*Just passing souls, no time to rest.*

Under the golden sun's soft gaze,

what do we find at the end of our days?

Generations come and generations go,

fleeting shadows wandering to and fro.

But Earth, in silent serenade,

and the ceaseless flow of hours and days

holds firm her ancient steady stance,

and bear her witness to our fleeting dance.

*The Sun's ballet from dawn to dusk,*

*is life's eternal, cyclic thrust.*

*The winds keep flitting: first south, then north,*

*in a rhythmic waltz, endlessly back and forth.*

*Rivers into great seas vent,*

*but their thirst never seems content.*

*They return as rain where they began before,*

*an eternal dance, forevermore.*

The world is full of wearying chores,

till our eyes and ears cannot bear much more.

From morning to night, too many to count.

An endless mountain, too steep to mount.

There's nothing new, it has all been done.

We constantly move to the same old song;

There's nothing new, it's all been seen before,

an endless desert, an endless shore.

In Jerusalem's heart, I stopped and stood.

to seek the truth in solitude.

I have no past, no future too,

just mired in this eternal dance we do.

Throughout my life I've seen it all,

futile chases, desires that fall.

Crooked lines that won't align,

in this vast design of time.

Into wisdom's depths I try to dive,

but am entrenched in madness, barely alive.

With every truth I seem to find,

the shadows lengthen: I am losing my mind.

For wisdom's gift is double-edged,

and joy and sorrow are intertwined.

The more you see, the more you fall;

the more you fathom the futility of it all.

Chapter 2

Meditation on **The Quest for Lasting Happiness**

*In pursuing the delightful, I dared to dance with decadence.*

*Yet, in the end, I was filled with ennui and despair.*

*Laughter? It's just a mere diversion.*

*And pleasure, that fickle guest, leaves no lasting mark.*

*I built mansions, cultivated vineyards,*

*designed gardens that bloomed with nature's poetry,*

*amassed fortunes and curated treasures:*

*the finest collections and luxuries were my every day.*

I sipped from every chalice of desire and took delight in each labor,

yet a haunting emptiness echoed back.

And now, reflecting upon those grand successes,

they seem no more substantial than a flirtation with the breeze.

*Wisdom, my dear, gleams like candlelight,*

*making folly's shadow seem all the more profound.*

*Yet, an unsettling truth soon emerged:*

*both the sage and the simpleton dance to the same final tune.*

The brilliant and the banal, alas,

are but stars in the night, destined to fade

Such vexation with life's grand tapestry!

What art I craft, what legacy I weave.

Who shall admire it once I've exited the stage?

*Perhaps our only true luxury*

*is to relish each day's task and sip the wine of contentment.*

*Such is the Divine's most enigmatic gift.*

*To those in His good graces, wisdom and joy are lavished.*

*But for those who wander?*

*They are merely trustees of treasures for the next fortunate soul.*

# Chapter 3

Meditation on **The Importance of the Present**

*For all, there's a season,*

*a perfect earthly reason.*

*A moment of birth, of death's quiet sigh,*

*a dawn of new, an evening goodbye.*

*A time to shield, a time to yield,*

*walls to crumble, dreams to build.*

Tears may fall, laughter might rise,

in grief's shadow, joy's surprise.

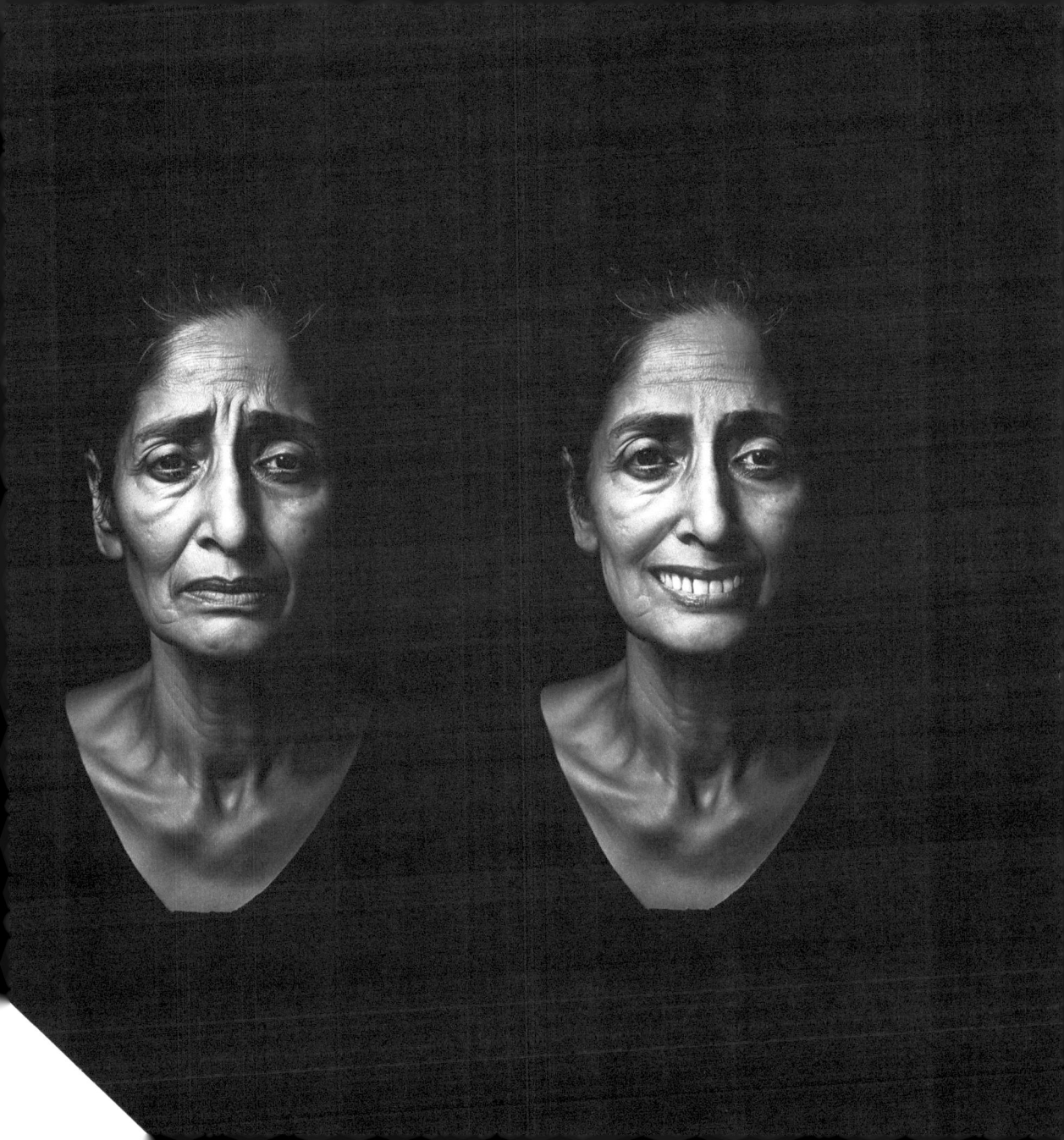

*A time for stones to fly, and then to gather,*

*to embrace near, or wander yonder.*

*A time to quest, a pause to rest,*

*hands to clasp, memories to cast.*

*A moment to fracture, a moment to stitch,*

*to hold one's tongue, or let words enrich.*

*To cherish, to scorn;*

*amidst strife, peace is born.*

*What fruits does our toil bear?*

*I've come to know the deeds that ensnare.*

All unfolds in destined rhyme;

the grand tapestry eludes every time.

Savor life's wine and its sunlit prime.

In labor's embrace, joy intertwines.

All that unfolds is but history's echo;

what will be has been, in time's endless flow.

*Elohim beckons, a reverent plea,*

*a call for justice, a promise to be.*

*Yet shadows loom in fairness's guise,*

*and in hallowed halls, injustice lies.*

*Elohim's trials, our souls they test,*

*unveiling our worst and unveiling our best.*

*Man and beast, our fate's the same,*

*a fleeting dance, life's ephemeral flame.*

*From dust to dust, the cycle repeats,*

*and beyond an enigma that we all must meet.*

*Beyond life's curtain, the unknown lurks certain.*

*Savor the now while there's time,*

*for tomorrow's sun might not shine.*

Chapter 4

Meditation on **The Value of Companionship**

In the city's gentle hum,

I beheld sorrows that bloomed when the sunlight was done.

Victims weep, power prevails; no solace, only despair.

And in this dance of sorrow, comfort seems rare.

Earth's heartaches are hidden from every gaze;

those who have left the stage

rest in silence 'neath the soft, earthen glaze.

More peaceful still are those unborn,

thankfully ignorant of life's bitter jest;

until they emerge into the turbulent world,

they are luckier than us in their silent rest.

Ambition, lit by jealousy's ember,

chases dreams that fade and dismember.

Inaction is the most self-harming art,

but peace sings a lullaby to the weary heart.

In solitude's grasp, a darker void I find,

alone, with yearnings to which my heart does cleave.

"For whom do I toil, life's joy left behind?"

In whispers lost, this soul does grieve.

In union, strength does lie.

When one stumbles, a friend's hand is dear.

Two can better stand against the tide,

if they fall, they can rise, side by side.

In adversity, united they stand,

secure in embrace, facing the storm.

Alone, one may fall, but two stand firm,

and a trio's bond is not easily torn.

The audacity of youth outshines the grey of old;

journeys can be made from obscurity to the throne.

The sun of today is tomorrow's eclipse.

Such is life, with its ever-changing scripts.

*In sacred halls, walk with mindful care.*

*Seek the heart, not just the ritual's glare.*

*For the Divine cherishes a genuine song,*

*more than ceaseless chants, where souls might go wrong.*

# Chapter 5

Meditation on **The Transience of Wealth and the Wisdom of Silence**

*In Jerusalem's ancient alleys, silence speaks before words.*

*He is in the vastness above; we in the narrow streets below.*

*Let our whispers be few.*

Dreams are woven from the threads of our worries.

Empty promises and many words are vanishing smoke.

Talk less, feel more.

If you pledge your word by the Eternals' name,

let it be done swiftly.

Better a silent heart than a broken vow.

*When you see the weak burdened and justice twisted,*

*Do not be disheartened for over every monarch*

*a higher sovereign reigns.*

The pursuit of gold, a thirst unquenched,

is like chasing mirages in the desert.

The more you possess, the more it's consumed by others.

What gain is there to the keeper, save the sight of his treasures?

The worker finds sweet rest after toil,

but abundance robs the rich of sleep

like a thief in the night.

A sorrowful sight I've witnessed: wealth accumulated,

only to harm its keeper or be lost to misfortune.

He is left empty-handed.

*As you came from the womb, so shall you return,*

*bereft, your hands empty, the fruits of your toil blown away.*

*There will be nothing to show.*

*Life is a puzzle.*

*No matter how much we toil and strive, it ends in nothing,*

*no more than footprints on the shore.*

*Take joy in life's simple things, for these are the gifts that life brings.*

*The Divine's gifts are to cherish.*

*Let one's heart not dwell on fleeting days*

*but fill it instead with joy.*

Chapter 6

Meditation on **The Search for True Joy**

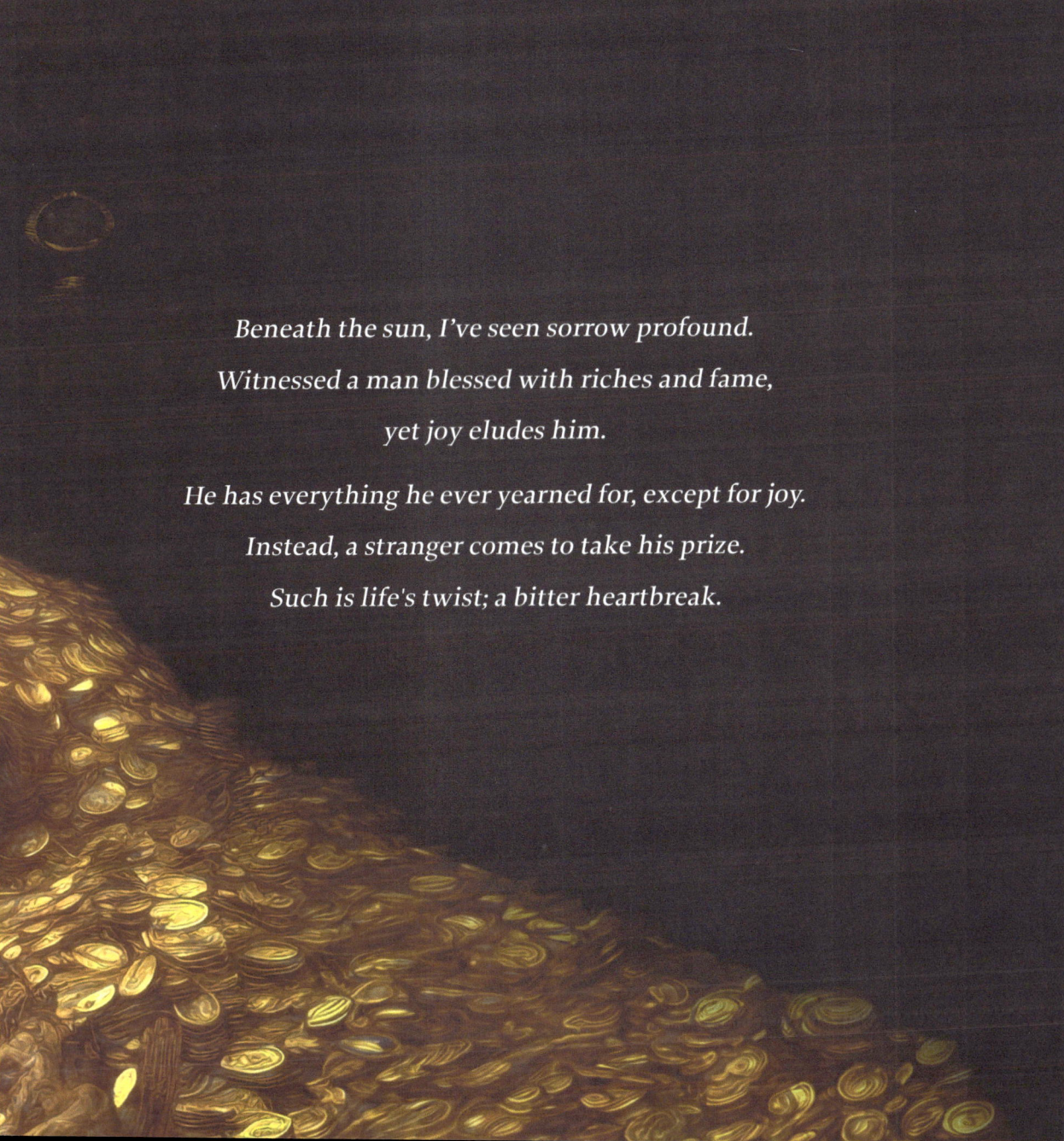

Beneath the sun, I've seen sorrow profound.
Witnessed a man blessed with riches and fame,
yet joy eludes him.

He has everything he ever yearned for, except for joy.
Instead, a stranger comes to take his prize.
Such is life's twist; a bitter heartbreak.

*If a man with a hundred children lives long years*
*but with no contentment or joy,*
*would it not be better to have never been born?*

*The stillborn child, in serenity comes forth.*
*It witnesses not the sun, nor pain of life;*
*in tranquil darkness, all feeling fades.*

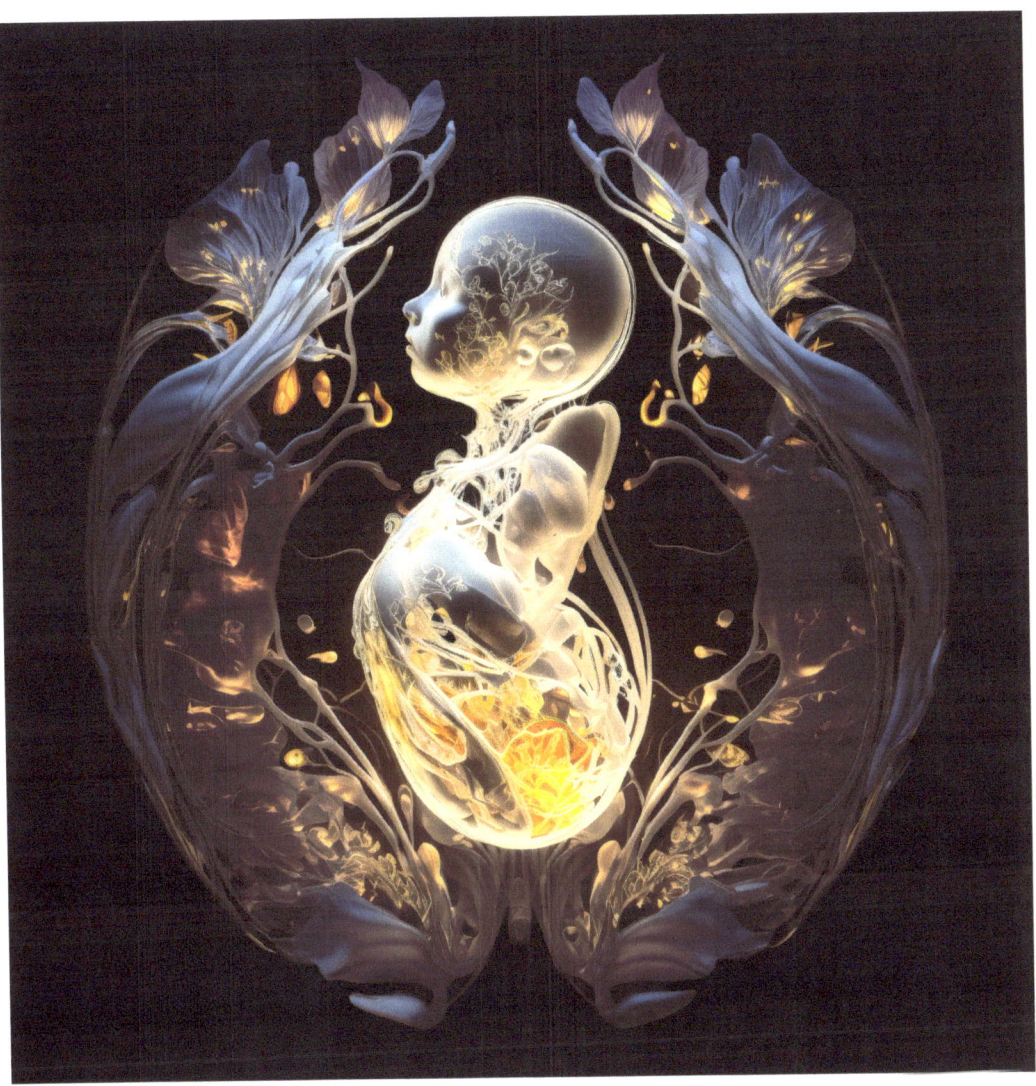

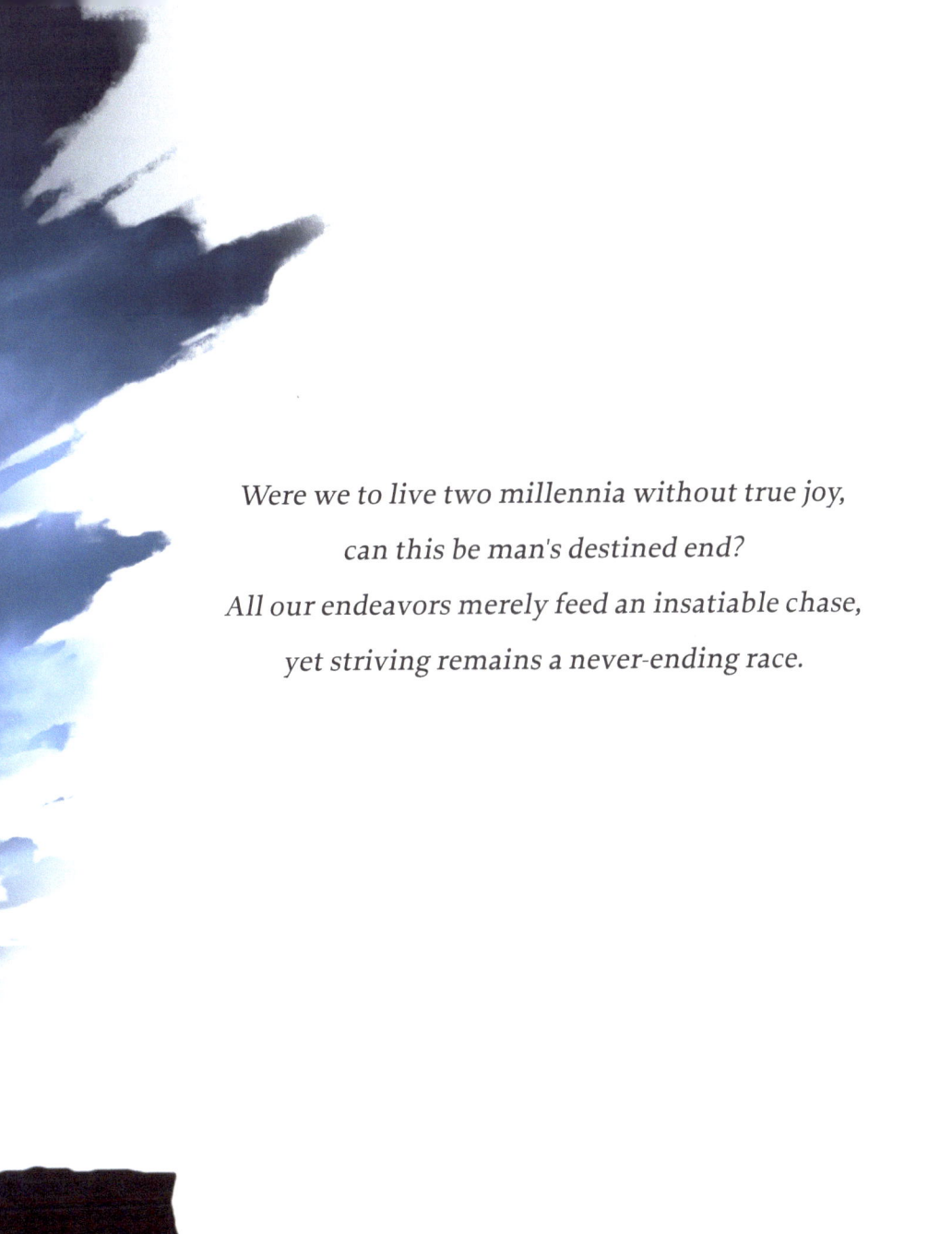

Were we to live two millennia without true joy,

can this be man's destined end?

All our endeavors merely feed an insatiable chase,

yet striving remains a never-ending race.

Truly, what has a wise man more than a fool?

Is a poor man's knowledge a valuable tool?

Better to trust in what's real, what is within one's sight,

than chase after desires that are as fleeting as the night.

*From birth to death, what real gain do we earn?*

*Who knows man's value as life's pages turn?*

*Who can predict his legacy or his final song?*

*What remains of a man once he is gone?*

Chapter 7

Meditation on **Embracing Life's Imperfections**

A person's good name surpasses fragrant oils that fade,
and death's quiet moment overshadows a newborn's first breath.

Walk the quiet lanes with mourners, heads hung low,
instead of raucous taverns.
The same end awaits us all.
The living must remember the echo
of their own footsteps along that road.

A furrowed brow speaks more than joy's fleeting tide,

for in the depths of worry, true feelings reside.

The thoughtful individual lingers in sorrow's shadow,

while the thoughtless bask in daylight, oblivious to impending gloom.

Heed the sage's words rather than the fool's hollow compliment,

for wisdom's admonition is more instructive than a fool's adoration.

The fool's laugh?

Like dry thistles crackling in a hot pan.

Fleeting, like the desert wind.

Greed's lure can tempt the sharpest mind.

A bribe, like a river, erodes the strongest of stones.

*Endings offer richer tales than introductions.*

*Tranquility reveals more depth than chaos.*

*Don't romanticize the past; true presence lies in the current moment.*

*With wisdom comes affluence, benefiting all under the heavens,*

*as a tree's shade offers comfort and its roots a haven.*

*The wise person finds a good life in knowledge's embrace,*

*while money, like a fleeting shadow, offers but a moment's grace.*

I've seen saints fall while sinners stand tall.

Life's a strange dance where none know all the steps.

Seek not purity absolute, nor wisdom's peak,

for in excess, even virtue blinds.

Delve not too deep in vice, nor play the fool.

Grasp the good and the ill, balance them in hand,

for one finds the way through both

as we traverse life's uncertain land.

*Perfection is but a mirage; every soul has its scar,*

*and even stars flicker and wane.*

*Before you judge others, hold a mirror up to your heart,*

*you might find your own stories reflected in theirs.*

*Haven't we all whispered regrets in solitude?*

*Haven't we all judged others while our own hands bear stains?*

*In my soul's journey, I have celebrated, reflected, and mourned,*

*struggling to find meaning amid life's turbulence.*

*Yet still my life danced out of reach,*

*an ever-shifting horizon, an ever-fleeting dream.*

Sexual lust captivates the restless mind.

Passions are deeper than canyons

that are rife with traps and treacheries

and riskier than any river's bend.

Living, with its desires, its love, and its strife

is the dance, the dream, the song, the life.

# Chapter 8

# Meditation on **Embracing Wisdom Amidst Life's Uncertainties**

Who among us can know every tale, every riddle, every plight?

Wisdom, like a candle's gleam,

brings a soft smile, a quiet dream.

*If to the heavens you made a vow*

*to stand by the sovereign,*

*then you must keep it now.*

*Rise not swiftly 'gainst the autocrat,*

*nor question when his gaze is down.*

*His word flows like a river's course:*

*steadfast, unyielding, with silent force.*

*Walk with him; avoid the snare;*

*wisdom is in the when and where.*

Life is an ever-turning wheel,

yet the morrow's secret, to no one, is revealed.

There is not one person who can predict tomorrow's sun

nor state with certainty when our days will be done.

No command have we over death's looming shade,

or in battles fierce, when plans are waylaid.

Evil's cloak is thin, offering no place to hide.

In life's hard trials, our courage is tried.

I've seen the wicked honored while good people look on.

I've seen good men wronged while the wicked roam free.

Criminals thrive, untouched, unscathed, alive:

by what right do they see the day and thrive?

Sinners live long, in spite of the tale

that goodness finds joy, and evil grows pale.

When justice seems to turn a blind eye,

it tempts the heart to give crime a try.

*So grasp at life's joy, hold it close, hold it dear;*

*find good cheer and seek love; eat and drink amidst fear.*

*Thus we endure this life on earth*

*given by the Divine, from the moment of birth.*

At night I ponder the world as it spins.

I seek the truth, yet to my chagrin,

that which unfolds, by chance or design

will remain an enigma for me for all time.

We may see what unfolds, by design or by chance;

but no matter how wise, we won't grasp life's secret dance.

# Chapter 9

Meditation on **Cherishing Life Amidst the Universe's Indifference**

In the vast sprawl of the universe,

I've come to realize

that, be we wise or simple,

fate's winds blow indiscriminately on us.

We all tread a similar path

that doesn't distinguish between the righteous and the wayward,

or those who bow in prayer or those who stray.

*There's a deep unfairness in the universe.*

*We live, we dance, we falter, we shine,*

*then, like candles, fade in the quiet night.*

*But in breathing, there's hope.*

*A scrappy, street-smart dog has more tales to tell*

*than a lion forever stilled.*

*We who breathe at least know of endings.*

*But the silent? They've parted from the sun and the rain.*

*Their stories are sealed.*

*All those fervent emotions – love, hate, envy –*

*melt like last winter's snow.*

*They won't partake in tomorrow's song.*

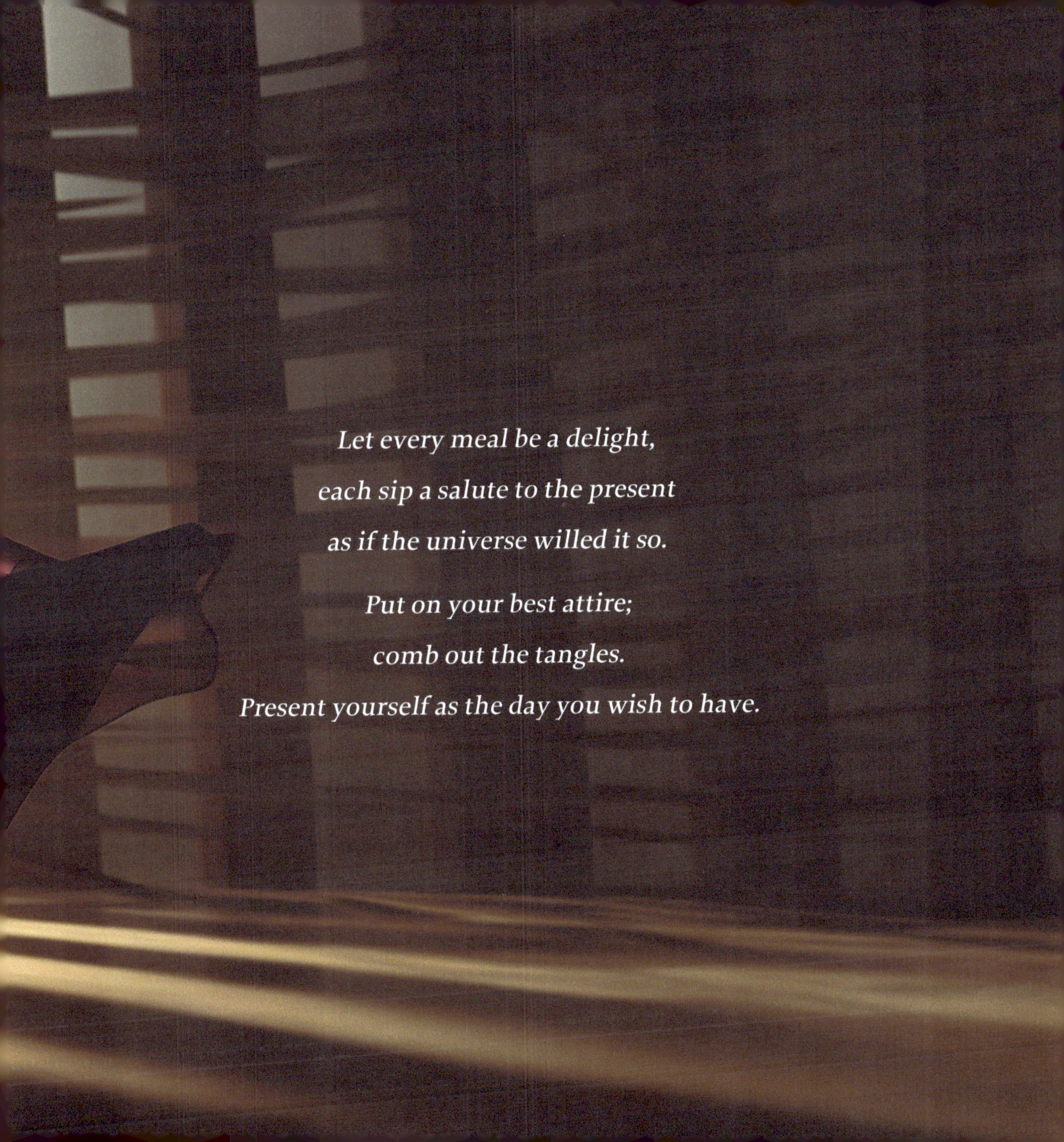

Let every meal be a delight,

each sip a salute to the present

as if the universe willed it so.

Put on your best attire;

comb out the tangles.

Present yourself as the day you wish to have.

*Embrace your lover, let it last.*

*Feel the pulse of desire, the joy of a kiss.*

*Feel the rhythm that leads one to bliss.*

*Engage earnestly in life's labor,*

*for there's silence in death*

*where thought and deed find no trace.*

Know this: Life's race isn't always to the swift,

nor the battle to the mightiest.

Even the wise and privileged falter in their stride.

We walk, often blind

to the hourglass's dwindling sands,

ensnared, much like fish caught unaware or birds trapped mid-flight.

I once glimpsed how fleeting our respect for wisdom is.

A tale of a small town, shadows of conquest looming,
yet it stood resilient, thanks to one poor person who saved the day
but was soon forgotten.

Therein, I found my answer.
Wisdom, subtle yet profound, outweighs brute force.
Nevertheless, the unassuming wise, if lacking gold or title,
often leave this world unseen.

Wisdom may stand tall and grand,

mightier than any warrior's hand.

Yet, a misstep, slight and unplanned,

can make it crumble like shifting sand.

# Chapter 10

Meditation on **Mindfulness in Thoughts, Words and Actions**

In spaces where fine scents are bottled and sealed,

there's a fly, a tiny intruder.

So small: yet it leaves its mark.

As does folly

when it comes to rest

amidst shining moments of wisdom.

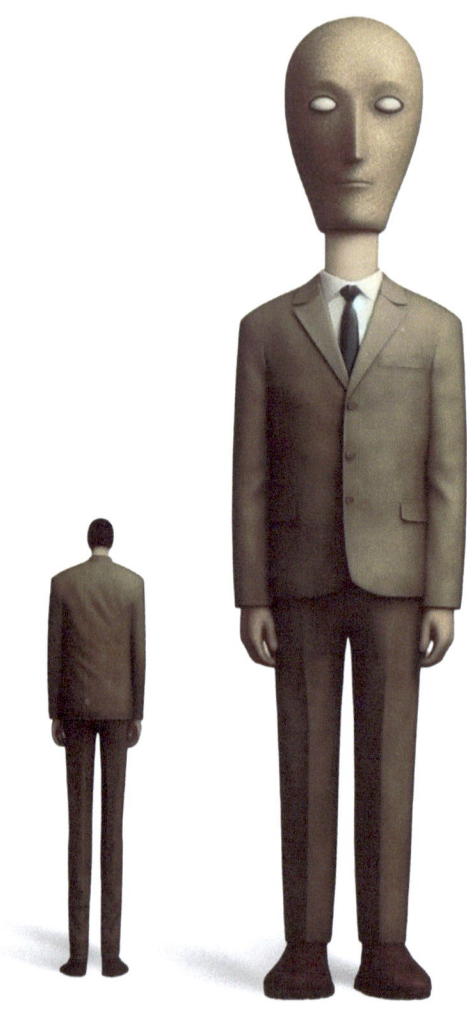

Those with clear minds,

are drawn to the first glimmers of day.

Others, ensnared by the mire of folly,

are swallowed by introspective nights as they lay.

Can you catch it?

That unmistakable tread of folly?

It resounds, betraying itself with each echoing motion.

Thoughtful words attract,

while thoughtless chatter risks alienation.

A fool's words, beginning in triviality,

into chaos can cascade.

Fools exhaust themselves in their ignorance,

wandering – aimless, lost – even on paths well laid.

In the world of authoritarians, strange imbalances lie.

Fools are celebrated while the worthy are brushed aside.

Stand your ground and keep your honor when the boss's tempers rise.

It is in patience that forgiveness finds its prize.

There is a new world where the chained rise above,

and their masters walk in the dust under the burning sun.

Be wary when you dig deep in this land.

One moment, you're standing, and the next, what do you find?

That you are inside the pit, looking out.

When walls are torn down, shadows might lurk behind.

Neglect, born from laziness, can lead a house to ruin;

overlook the trifling, and the entirety might suffer.

The act of creation isn't always something good.

Whether carving stone or splitting wood,

an ax, when sharp, cuts effortlessly,

just as a keen intellect can navigate life's intricacies.

A population risks instability when steered by impetuous leaders,

where frivolity overshadows obligation.

Yet, where wisdom steers the ship;

prosperity graces the nation.

Beware of the captivating.

Even a charmed serpent might surprise.

What use is its allure

if it turns to bite you between the eyes?

Feasts? They're a celebration, a heart's dance.

But the secret handshake, the whispered deal?

That's another dance,

slower, hidden, yet just as real.

Choose your words with the care of a craftsman.

The winds have a way of catching whispers.

And the birds?

They are ever-watchful listeners.

# Chapter 11

Meditation on **Embracing the Fleeting Nature of Youth**

*Cast your wealth as bread onto the water;*

*it shall return to you over time.*

*Share with the many your means and your care;*

*for a time may come when you'll need them to be there.*

As sure as clouds bring the rain to the ground,
actions have outcomes, and their results are profound.

Hesitate too long, and opportunities may wane.
Seize the day, or miss potential gain.

*We can't understand everything, like a child's first gasp;*

*so too, the Divine's ways are challenging to grasp.*

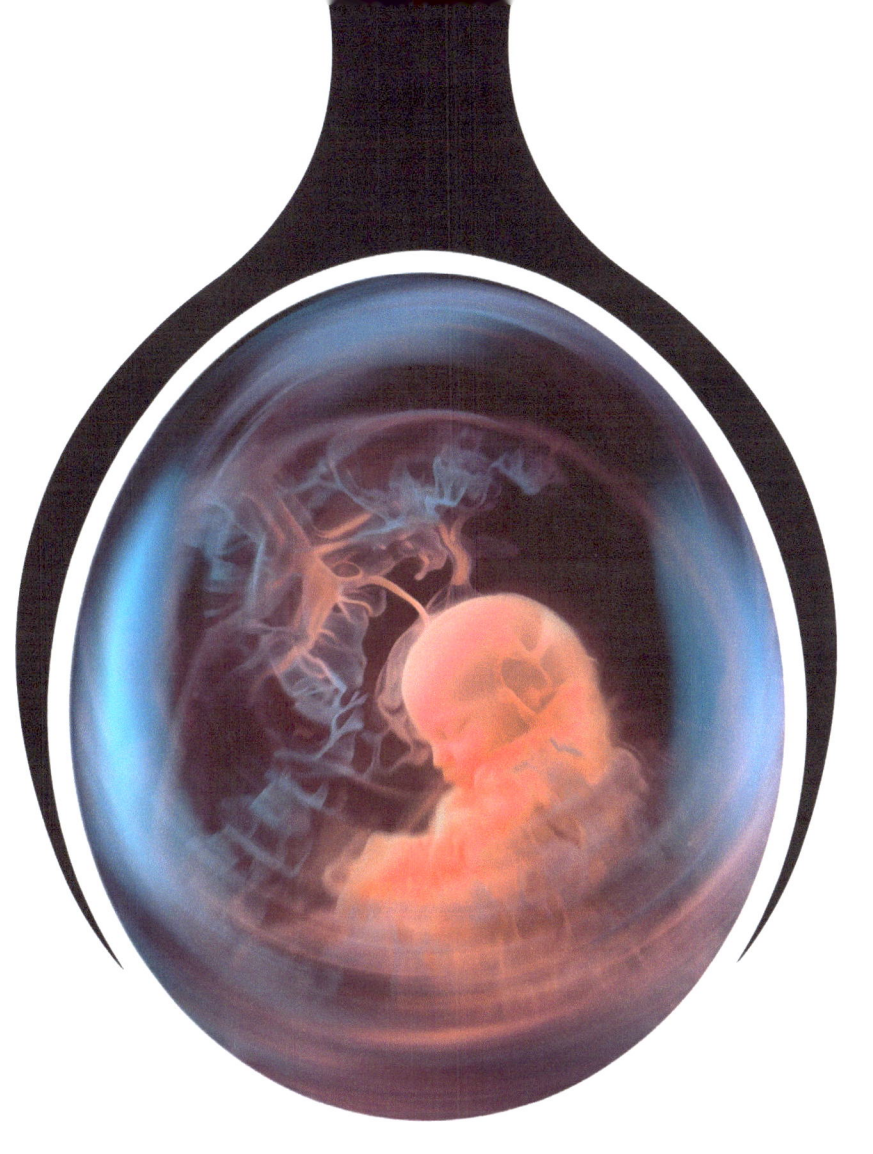

Dawn's gentle light is a beauty so true,
among Earth's finest sights, it forever renews.

Live fully each day, no matter your age,
eventually, a long, unknowable darkness awaits.

*Embrace the joys of youth and pursue your passions,*

*but remember that there is a consequence for every action.*

*Release worries, let go of the strain you clasp.*

*Cherish the fleeting moments of youth while it is still in your grasp.*

Chapter 12

# Meditation on **Aging and Mortality**

## Epilogue: A narrative of old age

Remember your Creator in days of youth yore,

Perhaps in time, you might say, with a weary brow,

"I don't enjoy life anymore."

A day will dawn when sun, moon, and stars seem like a distant haze

or like forgotten memories from bygone days.

Rain clouds might linger, casting shade,

dimming the world where once you played.

Your strength might waver, your eyes dim their gaze,
your teeth will weaken, and sights blur to a haze.

The vigor of youth is replaced by time's wear.
Echoes of past glories whisper, "Dare! Once more, dare!"

Hills once scaled, roads once tread,
now seem daunting, filled with dread.

Hair will turn silver, like the bloom of almond trees;
your once spry step becomes a languid breeze.

As grasshoppers age, slow down and become worn,
to our eternal homes, we're drawn, and regret fills the morn.

Life's fragile threads, silver and gold,
might break and snap, stories left untold.

The vessels of life, like pitchers of clay,
shatter and splinter in time's vast fray.

Our form returns to the ground, as it was at the start,
while the breath of life rejoins the Divine's heart.

Much I've observed, yet clarity's scant,

for life's vast tapestry is so wide and so vast.

As a teacher, I gathered wisdom, proverbs refined,

shared insights and truths for seekers to find.

I presented them with care, precision, and grace,

seeking the truest, most eloquent phrase.

Wisdom's words, like a shepherd's staff,

guide and direct and perhaps offer a path.

The Divine has bestowed us with His guiding light

to proceed through the day and understand the night.

Beware of false prophets, whose lies lead astray,

and focus on truths that can guide the way.

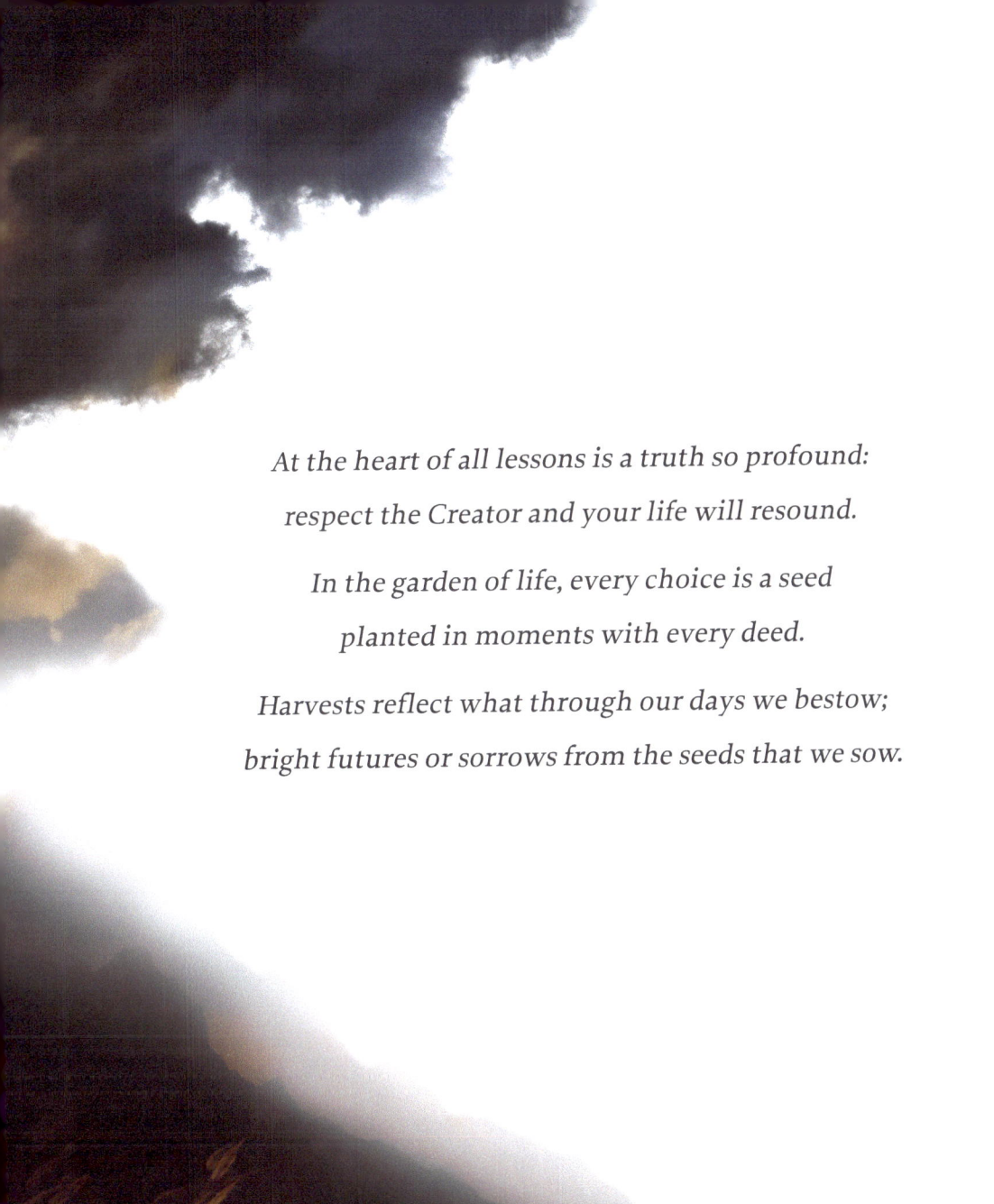

At the heart of all lessons is a truth so profound:
respect the Creator and your life will resound.

In the garden of life, every choice is a seed
planted in moments with every deed.

Harvests reflect what through our days we bestow;
bright futures or sorrows from the seeds that we sow.

## Photo credits

Cover | IStock Francescoch

22 | Silhouetted figure watch milk way: IStock Jesse Thompson

24 | Old City Jerusalem in Twilight: IStock Claudiad

30 | Ballerina Dancing with Silk Fabric: IStock inarik

62 | Lady Justice in barbed wire: IStock kemalbas

106 | Man Holding heavy weight: IStock Mohamed Ridi ROKI

132 | Lover stock illustration: IStock RussLyman

144 | Floris van Dyck 1575-1651

190 | Seascape at Dawn: IStock Elenaleonova

www.ingramcontent.com/pod-product-compliance
Lightning Source LLC
Chambersburg PA
CBHW041453120626
46547CB00003B/431

*9 7 9 8 2 1 8 3 9 6 3 4 3*